Nimble with Numbers

Student Practice Book

Grade 4

Leigh Childs and Laura Choate

Dale Seymour Publications®
Parsippany, New Jersey

Dale Seymour Publications
An imprint of Pearson Learning
299 Jefferson Road, P.O. Box 480
Parsippany, NJ 07054-0480

www.pearsonlearning.com

1-800-321-3106

Art Director: Jim O'Shea
Production/Manufacturing Director: Janet Yearian
Production/Manufacturing Manager: Karen Edmonds
Production/Manufacturing Coordinator: Julie Ryan
Editorial Manager: Elizabeth W. Fernald
Executive Editor: Amy Feldman

ISBN 0-7690-2821-7

4 5 6 7 8 9 10 - ML - 06 05 04

This Book Is Printed
On Recycled Paper

Table of Contents

Dear Student and Family,

What are some of your favorite things to do? A lot of fourth graders like to play video games or sports. But no matter what you like to do, you have to practice to get really good at it. Math is like that, too. You need to practice to get good at math.

This book is divided into five sections. Each section includes three kinds of activities to help you practice numbers—games, skill checks, and independent practice pages. You'll play games and solve puzzles while practicing addition, subtraction, multiplication, division, and fractions. The games in this book are intended to be used over and over. You may even play the same game four or five times while working in a section. You'll see that you get better at math each time you play.

You'll also do four skill checks in each section of the book. Date each one and complete them several days apart. These skill checks will help you, your teacher, and your family find out how you're doing. The independent practice pages in each section will help you work faster and do better. You'll practice numbers on your own and have fun at the same time. Be sure to find out how you did before moving on to the next practice page.

Soon you'll be a whiz with numbers—you just need to practice!

Yours truly,

Leigh Childs   *Laura Choate*

P.S. You'll need digit cards (on page 63) for most games and for some of the practice pages in this book. You might want to cut out the cards and save them to use over and over.

P.P.S. Here's a tip. Keep the cards in an envelope glued to the inside of your book.

Mixed Facts

Remember to play this game a few times. Your work often gets better when these games are played again a few days later.

Remember to date these Skill Checks so you can see improvement as you practice. The STOP activity helps you get ready for each Skill Check. Skill Check 1 should be done as you begin the section, and Skill Check 4 should be done as you end your work with this section.

These practice pages are designed to help you work faster and solve problems more accurately. Be sure to get feedback on how you're doing before starting another practice page.

Line-Ups Score

Warm-up
Roll three number cubes. Add, subtract, multiply, and/or divide the three numbers. Find four different answers. Explain.

Number of Players: 2

Goal: Cover the most numbers in a row.

Materials: *Line-Ups Score* gameboard (page 7)

3 number cubes

Markers in 2 colors (12 of each color)

Game Rules

1. The first player rolls the number cubes. That player adds, subtracts, multiplies, and/or divides the three numbers. The other player checks to make sure the answer is correct. The first player covers the answer on the gameboard.

   Example: The first player rolls 2, 3, and 5. The player says, "3 times 2 plus 5 equals 11" and covers 11 on the board.

2. Players take turns and try to cover neighboring numbers. If a player cannot make an answer match *any* uncovered number, the other player gets a chance. If neither player can make an answer that works, the first player loses that turn.

3. Play continues until both players use all of their markers.

4. Each player finds his or her score. The player with the greater score wins the game.

   3 in a row is 1 point
   4 in a row is 3 points
   5 in a row is 6 points

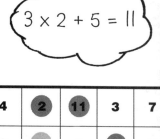

4	2	11	3	7
8	24	5	4	3
17	1	12	2	18
2	9	3	1	10
12	4	1	16	5

Make It Harder: Players roll four number cubes. They use 3 or 4 of the rolled numbers.

Don't Forget: Play the game over and over. It will help you do better on skill checks and independent practice pages.

Line-Ups Score

4	2	11	3	7
8	24	5	4	3
17	1	12	2	18
2	9	3	1	10
12	4	1	16	5

Date _____

Skill Check 1

 Don't start yet! Star problems in the top row that may have odd answers.

1. $\begin{array}{r} 8 \\ \times 7 \\ \hline \end{array}$

2. $4\overline{)32}$

3. $15 \div 3 =$ _____

4. $(56 \div 8) \times (45 \div 5) =$ _____

5. $(45 \div 9) + 8 =$ _____

6. $(12 \div 2) \times (17 - 9) =$ _____

7. $(4 \times 3) + 5 =$ ___

8. Use 5, 3, and 2.

$(\square + \square) \times \square = 25$

9. Use 2, 4, and 6.

$(\square \times \square) \div \square = 12$

10. Use 3, 6, and 9.

$(\square \div \square) \times \square = 18$

Go On ▶ Using at least two operations, write three equations that equal 17.

Date _____

Skill Check 2

 Don't start yet! Star a problem that may have the greatest answer.

1. $\begin{array}{r} 7 \\ \times 6 \\ \hline \end{array}$

2. $9\overline{)27}$

3. $30 \div 5 =$ _____

4. $(48 \div 6) \times (40 \div 8) =$ _____

5. $(49 \div 7) + 9 =$ _____

6. $(28 \div 7) \times (14 - 8) =$ _____

7. $(3 \times 6) - 4 =$ _____

8. Use 3, 4, and 5.

$(\square + \square) \times \square = 27$

9. Use 3, 5, and 6.

$(\square \times \square) \div \square = 10$

10. Use 2, 6, and 8.

$(\square \div \square) \times \square = 24$

 Use any four digits to complete each equation.

$(\square \times \square) - (\square \div \square) = 12$ $(\square \times \square) \div (\square + \square) = 3$

Position Facts A

Write the missing numbers. A sample problem is done for you.

Sample:

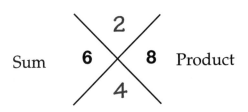

Sum   **6**   **8**   Product

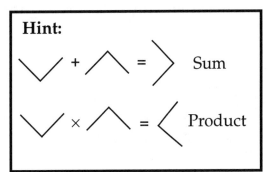

1.

10   16   8   7   9   18   9   14   11   18

2.

16   63   17   72   13   40   13   36   16   64

3.

  3   4   3   5   4

6   10   8   7   9

Fun Fact: The sum of all numbers filled in for row 3 above equals the greatest 2-digit number.

4.

15   48   14   7   49   81

6   6   5   9

Challenge: Create two puzzles for your classmates to solve. Then try them with a partner.

Possible Equations A

Numbers: 1, 2, 3, 6

Add, subtract, multiply, and/or divide any three of these numbers to complete the equations.

□ ○ □ ○ □ = 1

□ ○ □ ○ □ = 7

□ ○ □ ○ □ = 2

□ ○ □ ○ □ = 8

□ ○ □ ○ □ = 3

□ ○ □ ○ □ = 9

□ ○ □ ○ □ = 4

□ ○ □ ○ □ = 10

□ ○ □ ○ □ = 5

□ ○ □ ○ □ = 11

□ ○ □ ○ □ = 6

□ ○ □ ○ □ = 12

Independent Activity

Joining Neighbors A

Use at least three neighboring numbers and more than one operation to equal the indicated target numbers. Loop the numbers used on the grids. Record the equations. Remember to use parentheses when necessary. The first one is done for you.

1. $2 \times 6 \div 4 = 3$ _____

2. _____

3. _____

4. _____

5. _____

6. _____

7. _____

8. _____

9. _____

10. _____

11. _____

12. _____

Date _____

Skill Check 3

 Don't start yet! Star problems that may have even answers.

1. 9
  × 6

2. 4⟌24

3. 18 ÷ 3 = _____

4. (54 ÷ 9) × (63 ÷ 7) = _____

5. (42 ÷ 7) + 9 = _____   **6.** (21 ÷ 3) × (13 − 9) = _____   **7.** (6 × 4) − 2 = _____

8. Use 2, 4, and 5.

(☐ + ☐) × ☐ = 28

9. Use 4, 6, and 9.

(☐ × ☐) ÷ ☐ = 6

10. Use 2, 4, and 6.

(☐ ÷ ☐) × ☐ = 12

Go On ▶ Using at least two operations, write three equations that equal 27.

_____

Date _____

Skill Check 4

 Don't start yet! Star a problem in the top row that may have the least answer.

1. 8
  × 8

2. 4⟌36

3. 42 ÷ 6 = _____

4. (63 ÷ 9) × (56 ÷ 7) = _____

5. (36 ÷ 4) + 8 = _____   **6.** (35 ÷ 5) × (13 − 7) = _____   **7.** (3 × 5) + 4 = _____

8. Use 3, 4, and 5.

(☐ + ☐) × ☐ = 32

9. Use 4, 6, and 8.

(☐ × ☐) ÷ ☐ = 3

10. Use 4, 8, and 8.

(☐ ÷ ☐) × ☐ = 16

 Go On Use any four digits to complete each equation.

(☐ × ☐) − (☐ ÷ ☐) = 7   (☐ × ☐) ÷ (☐ + ☐) = 8

Position Facts B

Write the missing numbers. A sample problem is done for you.

Sample:

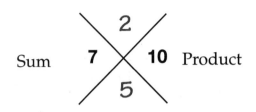

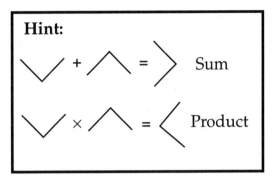

1.

2.

   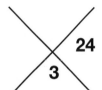 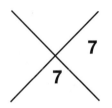

Fun Fact: The sum of all numbers filled in for row 2 above equals the last two digits of the year the Declaration of Independence was signed.

3.

 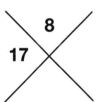 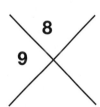 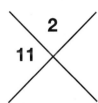

4.

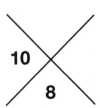

Challenge: Create two puzzles for your classmates to solve. Then try them with a partner.

Possible Equations B

Numbers: 2, 3, 5, 6

Add, subtract, multiply, and/or divide any three of these numbers to complete the equations. **Hint:** A solution may not be possible for each equation.

☐ ○ ☐ ○ ☐ = 1   ☐ ○ ☐ ○ ☐ = 9

☐ ○ ☐ ○ ☐ = 2   ☐ ○ ☐ ○ ☐ = 10

☐ ○ ☐ ○ ☐ = 3   ☐ ○ ☐ ○ ☐ = 12

☐ ○ ☐ ○ ☐ = 4   ☐ ○ ☐ ○ ☐ = 14

☐ ○ ☐ ○ ☐ = 6   ☐ ○ ☐ ○ ☐ = 16

☐ ○ ☐ ○ ☐ = 7   ☐ ○ ☐ ○ ☐ = 17

Independent Activity

Joining Neighbors B

Use at least three neighboring numbers and more than one operation to equal the indicated target numbers. Loop the numbers used on the grids. Record the equations. Remember to use parentheses when necessary.

1. _____

2. _____

3. _____

4. _____

5. _____

6. _____

7. _____

8. _____

9. _____

10. _____

11. _____

12. _____

Possible Equations C

Numbers: 2, 3, 4, 8

Add, subtract, multiply, and/or divide any three of these numbers to complete the equations.

$\square \bigcirc \square \bigcirc \square = 1$

$\square \bigcirc \square \bigcirc \square = 9$

$\square \bigcirc \square \bigcirc \square = 2$

$\square \bigcirc \square \bigcirc \square = 10$

$\square \bigcirc \square \bigcirc \square = 3$

$\square \bigcirc \square \bigcirc \square = 12$

$\square \bigcirc \square \bigcirc \square = 4$

$\square \bigcirc \square \bigcirc \square = 15$

$\square \bigcirc \square \bigcirc \square = 5$

$\square \bigcirc \square \bigcirc \square = 16$

$\square \bigcirc \square \bigcirc \square = 7$

$\square \bigcirc \square \bigcirc \square = 18$

Independent Activity

Addition and Subtraction

Remember to play this game a few times. Your work often gets better when these games are played again a few days later.

Remember to date these Skill Checks so you can see improvement as you practice. The STOP activity helps you get ready for each Skill Check. Skill Check 5 should be done as you begin the section, and Skill Check 8 should be done as you end your work with this section.

These practice pages are designed to help you work faster and solve problems more accurately. Be sure to get feedback on how you're doing before starting another practice page.

Reach the Peak

Warm-up
Look at the problems in the bottom row of the gameboard on page 19. Find the missing digit for one problem. Explain your thinking.

Number of Players: 2

Goal: Travel from the bottom to the top of the peak.

Materials: 2 sets of digit cards (4–9 only)
Reach the Peak gameboard (page 19)
2 different markers (one for each player)

Game Rules

1. Mix the 2 sets of cards and place them face-down in a pile.

2. The first player turns over the top card. The player looks at the bottom row of the gameboard to find a problem missing that digit. The player explains how that digit completes the problem and covers the problem with his or her marker.

3. The other player takes a turn, also working in the bottom row of the gameboard. If necessary, both players may put their markers on the same problem.

4. For the remaining turns, players can *only* move their marker to a neighboring problem. So, if the selected digit is missing from a neighboring problem, the player can move to that space. If not, the player stays put.

5. The first player to reach the problem at the top of the peak wins the game.

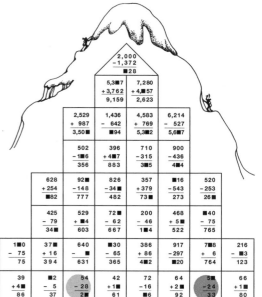

Make It Harder: Each player uses two markers but moves only one marker on a turn. The player who reaches the top with one marker wins.

Reach the Peak

$$\begin{array}{r} 2,000 \\ -1,372 \\ \hline \blacksquare 28 \end{array}$$

$\begin{array}{r} 5,3\blacksquare7 \\ +3,762 \\ \hline 9,159 \end{array}$	$\begin{array}{r} 7,280 \\ +4,\blacksquare57 \\ \hline 2,623 \end{array}$

$\begin{array}{r} 2,529 \\ +\ 987 \\ \hline 3,50\blacksquare \end{array}$	$\begin{array}{r} 1,436 \\ -\ 642 \\ \hline \blacksquare94 \end{array}$	$\begin{array}{r} 4,583 \\ +\ 769 \\ \hline 5,3\blacksquare2 \end{array}$	$\begin{array}{r} 6,214 \\ -\ 527 \\ \hline 5,6\blacksquare7 \end{array}$
$\begin{array}{r} 502 \\ -1\blacksquare6 \\ \hline 356 \end{array}$	$\begin{array}{r} 396 \\ +4\blacksquare7 \\ \hline 883 \end{array}$	$\begin{array}{r} 710 \\ -315 \\ \hline 3\blacksquare5 \end{array}$	$\begin{array}{r} 900 \\ -436 \\ \hline 4\blacksquare4 \end{array}$

$\begin{array}{r} 628 \\ +254 \\ \hline \blacksquare82 \end{array}$	$\begin{array}{r} 92\blacksquare \\ -148 \\ \hline 777 \end{array}$	$\begin{array}{r} 826 \\ -34\blacksquare \\ \hline 482 \end{array}$	$\begin{array}{r} 357 \\ +379 \\ \hline 73\blacksquare \end{array}$	$\begin{array}{r} \blacksquare16 \\ -543 \\ \hline 273 \end{array}$	$\begin{array}{r} 520 \\ -253 \\ \hline 26\blacksquare \end{array}$
$\begin{array}{r} 425 \\ -\ 79 \\ \hline 34\blacksquare \end{array}$	$\begin{array}{r} 529 \\ +\ \blacksquare4 \\ \hline 603 \end{array}$	$\begin{array}{r} 72\blacksquare \\ -\ 62 \\ \hline 667 \end{array}$	$\begin{array}{r} 200 \\ -\ 46 \\ \hline 1\blacksquare4 \end{array}$	$\begin{array}{r} 468 \\ +\ 5\blacksquare \\ \hline 522 \end{array}$	$\begin{array}{r} \blacksquare40 \\ -\ 75 \\ \hline 765 \end{array}$

$\begin{array}{r} 1\blacksquare0 \\ -\ 75 \\ \hline 75 \end{array}$	$\begin{array}{r} 37\blacksquare \\ +\ 16 \\ \hline 394 \end{array}$	$\begin{array}{r} 640 \\ -\ \ \blacksquare \\ \hline 631 \end{array}$	$\begin{array}{r} \blacksquare30 \\ -\ 65 \\ \hline 365 \end{array}$	$\begin{array}{r} 386 \\ +\ 86 \\ \hline 4\blacksquare2 \end{array}$	$\begin{array}{r} 917 \\ -297 \\ \hline \blacksquare20 \end{array}$	$\begin{array}{r} 7\blacksquare8 \\ +\ \ 6 \\ \hline 764 \end{array}$	$\begin{array}{r} 216 \\ -\ \blacksquare3 \\ \hline 123 \end{array}$
$\begin{array}{r} 39 \\ +4\blacksquare \\ \hline 86 \end{array}$	$\begin{array}{r} \blacksquare2 \\ -\ 5 \\ \hline 37 \end{array}$	$\begin{array}{r} 54 \\ -\ 28 \\ \hline 2\blacksquare \end{array}$	$\begin{array}{r} 42 \\ +1\blacksquare \\ \hline 61 \end{array}$	$\begin{array}{r} 72 \\ -16 \\ \hline \blacksquare6 \end{array}$	$\begin{array}{r} 64 \\ +2\blacksquare \\ \hline 92 \end{array}$	$\begin{array}{r} 5\blacksquare \\ -24 \\ \hline 33 \end{array}$	$\begin{array}{r} 66 \\ +1\blacksquare \\ \hline 80 \end{array}$

Date _____

Skill Check 5

 Don't start yet. Star any problems in row 2 that may have odd answers.

1. $38 + 12 + 43 =$ ____   **2.** $100 - 28 =$ ____   **3.** $71 - 14 =$ ____

4. 562
   $- 86$

5. 684
   $+ 67$

6. 947
   $+ 373$

7. 608
   $- 159$

8. 1,342
   $- 555$

9. 5,160
   $- 2,446$

10. $200 - 156 =$ ____

 What number is missing? 746, 714, 682, _____ , 618
Describe your rule.

Date _____

Skill Check 6

 Don't start yet. Star four problems that may have answers less than 200.

1. $35 + 28 + 35 =$ ____   **2.** $100 - 19 =$ ____   **3.** $82 - 16 =$ ____

4. 483
   $- 92$

5. 727
   $+ 74$

6. 986
   $+ 464$

7. 802
   $- 246$

8. 1,463
   $- 777$

9. 4,286
   $- 2,357$

10. $200 - 165 =$ ____

 These are complete pairs: $27 + 73$, $45 + 55$, $32 + 68$.
Make each pair a complete pair. $30 +$ ____ , $64 +$ ____ , $71 +$ ____

Honeycomb Subtraction

Use the hexagon key and sample to determine how to find the missing numbers.

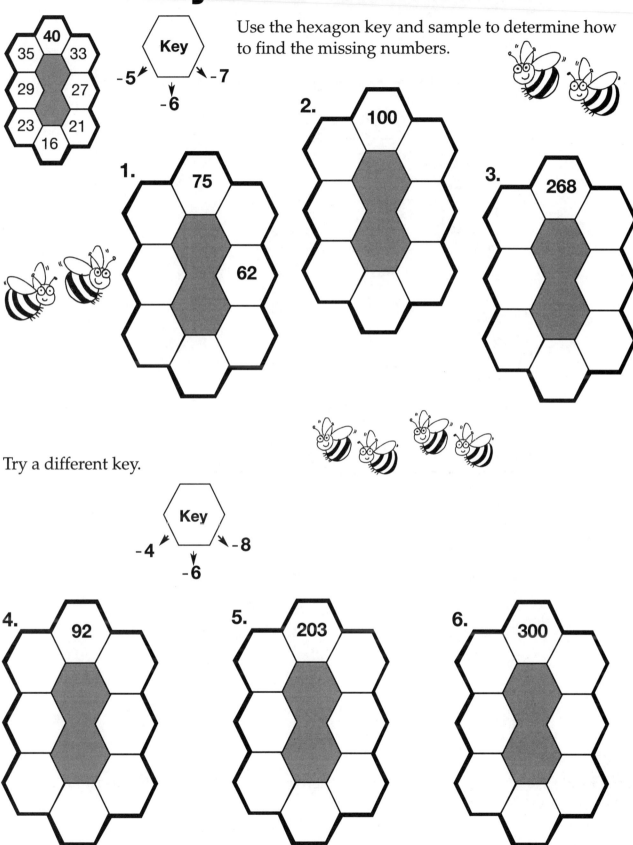

Try a different key.

Cross-Number Puzzle A

Use the clues to solve the puzzle.

Across
1. 265 + 443

4. 8,000 – 2,351

6. 671 + 169

7. 1,040 – 999

9. 1,622 – 688

11. 2,105 – 1,722

12. 88 + 698

Down
1. 5,864 + 1,460

2. 212 – 14

3. 18,565 + 13,511

5. 775 + 5,634

8. 9,213 – 8,070

10. 836 – 379

Fun Fact: The sum of "8 down" and "12 across" equals the year the car radio was invented.

Rearrange and Find A

Use digit cards 1–9 to help you solve the following problems.

| 2 4 5 9 | Use 3 of these digits and + or – to make each equation true.

1. ___ ___ ◯ ___ = 61

2. ___ ___ ◯ ___ = 37

3. ___ ___ ◯ 1 ___ = 79

4. ___ ___ ◯ ___ = 88

5. ___ ___ ◯ 6 ___ = 93

6. ___ ___ ◯ ___ 8 = 26

| 3 5 6 8 | Use all 4 digits and + or – to make each equation true.

7. ___ ___ ◯ ___ ___ = 94

8. ___ ___ ◯ ___ ___ = 18

9. ___ ___ ◯ ___ ⊖ ___ = 50

10. ___ ___ ◯ ___ ⊖ ___ = 55

11. ___ ___ ___ ◯ ___ = 544

12. ___ ___ ___ ◯ ___ = 357

| 2 6 7 9 | Use all 4 digits and + and/or – to make each equation true.

13. ___ ◯ ___ ◯ ___ ___ = 78

14. ___ ___ ◯ ___ ___ = 141

15. ___ ___ ◯ ___ ___ = 3

16. ___ ___ ◯ (___ ◯ ___) = 79

17. ___ ___ ◯ (___ ◯ ___) = 74

18. ___ ___ ◯ ___ ___ = 47

| 1 2 4 5 9 | Use 4 of these digits and + and/or – to make each equation true.

19. ___ ___ ___ ◯ ___ = 424

20. ___ ___ ◯ ___ ◯ ___ = 22

21. ___ ___ ◯ ___ ___ = 22

22. ___ ___ ___ ◯ ___ = 242

23. ___ ___ ___ ◯ ___ = 588

24. ___ ___ ◯ ___ ___ = 33

Date _____

Skill Check 7

 STOP Don't start yet. Star any problems that may have answers greater than 500.

1. $54 + 26 + 19 =$ ____   **2.** $100 - 24 =$ ____   **3.** $73 - 15 =$ ____

4. 527
    $- 59$

5. 667
    $+ 65$

6. 964
    $+ 388$

7. 703
    $- 135$

8. $1,236$
    $- 888$

9. $4,172$
    $- 2,233$

10. $200 - 137 =$ ____

Go On Write three different equations that equal 420. Describe your strategy.

Date _____

Skill Check 8

 STOP Don't start yet. Star the problem that may have the greatest answer.

1. $24 + 44 + 26 =$ ____   **2.** $100 - 16 =$ ____   **3.** $84 - 17 =$ ____

4. 424
    $- 66$

5. 748
    $+ 76$

6. 977
    $+ 464$

7. 905
    $- 246$

8. $1,337$
    $- 448$

9. $5,295$
    $- 2,368$

10. $200 - 142 =$ ____

 Go On Insert one addition sign and one subtraction sign to make this equation true. Describe your strategy.   3 4 6 8 5 2 7 9 = 540

Cross-Number Puzzle B

Use the clues to solve the puzzle.

Across

1. 900 – 175

5. 1,973 + 1,888

7. 548 + 59

8. 5,210 – 5,115

10. 1,000 – 21

11. 286 + 285

13. 571 + 357

14. 1,200 – 577

Down

1. 6,712 + 697

2. 1,001 – 948

3. 137 + 279

4. 34,879 + 47,862

6. 10,000 – 1,471

9. 8,105 – 2,136

12. 12,301 – 11,509

Fun Fact: The difference between "1 down" and "9 down" equals the number of minutes in one day.

Rearrange and Find B

Use digit cards 1–9 to help you solve the following problems.

2 3 6 9 Use all 4 digits and + and/or – to make each equation true.

1. ___ ___ ◯ ___ ___ = 101

2. ___ ___ ◯ ___ ___ = 56

3. ___ ___ ◯ ___ ___ = 92

4. ___ ___ ◯ ___ ___ = 23

5. ___ ___ ◯ ___ ◯ ___ = 74

6. ___ ___ ◯ (___ ◯ ___) = 83

---

3 4 5 9 Use all 4 digits and + or – to make each equation true.

7. ___ ___ ◯ ___ ___ = 48

8. ___ ___ ◯ (___ ⊗ ___) = 27

9. ___ ___ ⊖ ___ ◯ ___ = 58

10. ___ ___ ◯ (___ ⊗ ___) = 17

11. ___ ___ ◯ ___ ___ = 84

12. ___ ___ ⊗ (___ ◯ ___) = 98

13. ___ ___ ◯ (___ ⊗ ___) = 88

14. (___ ⊗ ___) ◯ ___ ___ = 113

---

1 3 5 6 8 Use 4 of these digits and any operation sign to make each equation true.

15. ___ ___ ◯ ___ ___ = 121

16. ___ ___ ◯ ___ ___ = 25

17. ___ ___ ◯ (___ ◯ ___) = 41

18. ___ ___ ◯ (___ ◯ ___) = 101

19. ___ ___ ◯ (___ ◯ ___) = 63

20. (___ ◯ ___) ◯ ___ ___ = 83

---

2 4 5 7 8 Use 4 or 5 of these digits and any operation sign to make each equation true.

21. ___ ___ ◯ ___ ___ = 14

22. ___ ___ ◯ (___ ◯ ___) = 57

23. (___ ___ ◯ ___) ◯ ___ = 110

24. ___ ___ ◯ ___ ___ = 82

25. (___ ◯ ___) ◯ ___ ___ = 89

26. ___ ___ ___ ◯ ___ ___ = 158

27. ___ ___ ___ ◯ (___ ◯ ___) = 396

28. ___ ___ ___ ◯ (___ ◯ ___) = 249

Independent Activity

Multiplication

Remember to play this game a few times. Your work often gets better when these games are played again a few days later.

Remember to date these Skill Checks so you can see improvement as you practice. The STOP activity helps you get ready for each Skill Check. Skill Check 9 should be done as you begin the section, and Skill Check 12 should be done as you end your work with this section.

These practice pages are designed to help you work faster and solve problems more accurately. Be sure to get feedback on how you're doing before starting another practice page.

Products Bingo

Number of Players: 4 (2 on each team)

Goal: Cover 3 in a row.

Materials: *Products Bingo* gameboard (page 29)
Markers in 2 colors (12 of each color)
Calculator (optional)

Game Rules

1. Team A picks one factor from each row in the Choices box. Players use pencil and paper or a calculator to find the product. Team A covers the product on the gameboard.

Example: Team A picks 7 and 51. They say "7 times 51" and find the product. They cover the product, 357, on the gameboard.

2. Teams take turns.

3. The first team to have three markers in a row wins the game. The row can go across, down, or diagonally.

Choices:				
3	4	5	7	9
22	39	51	76	84

Make It Harder: The winning team must have four markers in a row.

Don't Forget: Play this game over and over. It will help you do better on skill checks and independent practice pages.

66	88	110	117	153
154	156	195	198	204
228	252	255	273	304
336	351	357	380	420
459	532	588	684	756

$$\begin{array}{r} 51 \\ \times\ 7 \\ \hline 357 \end{array}$$

Products Bingo

Choices:

3	4	5	7	9
22	39	51	76	84

66	88	110	117	153
154	156	195	198	204
228	252	255	273	304
336	351	357	380	420
459	532	588	684	756

Game

Date _____

Skill Check 9

 Don't start yet. Star problems that may have answers greater than 1,000.

1. $60 \times 9 =$ _____

2. $310 \times 7 =$ _____

3. 44
$\underline{\times 8}$

4. 72
$\underline{\times 6}$

5. 58
$\underline{\times 5}$

6. $(4 \times 90) - 30 =$ _____

7. 453
$\underline{\times 3}$

8. 408
$\underline{\times 9}$

9. 39
$\underline{\times 40}$

10. $300 - (33 \times 3) =$ _____

 Use the digits 2, 3, 7, and 8 to write a multiplication equation with the greatest possible product. Describe your strategy.

Date _____

Skill Check 10

 Don't start yet. Star the problem in row 3 that may have the greatest answer.

1. $90 \times 8 =$ _____

2. $420 \times 3 =$ _____

3. 53
$\underline{\times 6}$

4. 65
$\underline{\times 5}$

5. 48
$\underline{\times 4}$

6. $(5 \times 80) - 60 =$ _____

7. 532
$\underline{\times 4}$

8. 705
$\underline{\times 6}$

9. 47
$\underline{\times 20}$

10. $400 - (43 \times 3) =$ _____

 What's missing? 80, 160, 240, 320, _____ , 480
Describe the pattern.

Finding Tic-Tac-Toes A

Complete the equations. Then find the tic-tac-toe for each grid. Find the row, column, or diagonal with three numbers matching answers from the equations.

1.

47	32	126
9	55	84
110	18	71

$100 - (9 \times 5) =$ _____ $12 + (19 \times 6) =$ _____

$(15 \times 3) + 2 =$ _____ $(12 \times 4) - 30 =$ _____

$(15 \times 6) - 6 =$ _____ $20 + (18 \times 5) =$ _____

2.

120	79	25
48	63	102
91	36	117

$(36 \times 3) - 6 =$ _____ $(5 \times 15) - 50 =$ _____

$(16 \times 5) - 32 =$ _____ $(4 \times 21) + 7 =$ _____

$(7 \times 17) - 40 =$ _____ $(18 \times 6) + 9 =$ _____

3.

52	19	124
67	81	73
132	46	100

$100 - (3 \times 27) =$ _____ $20 + (4 \times 28) =$ _____

$100 - (3 \times 18) =$ _____ $(6 \times 16) + 4 =$ _____

$(17 \times 5) - 18 =$ _____ $(3 \times 75) - 101 =$ _____

4.

96	115	87
38	129	104
161	127	95

$(19 \times 7) - 4 =$ _____ $(16 \times 9) + 17 =$ _____

$14 + (18 \times 5) =$ _____ $(6 \times 19) - 19 =$ _____

$(6 \times 17) - 6 =$ _____ $(5 \times 27) - 20 =$ _____

Fun Fact: The sum of all the answers for #4 equals the number of different words that the average 10-year-old uses in one hour.

Products Galore A

Arrange the factors to make each product. The first one is started for you.

1. Factors: 8, 10, 11, 12

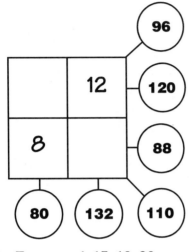

2. Factors: 11, 13, 14, 15

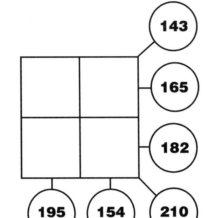

3. Factors: 7, 12, 14, 15

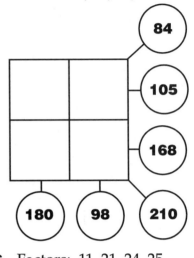

4. Factors: 6, 15, 19, 20

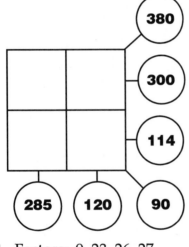

5. Factors: 9, 20, 21, 25

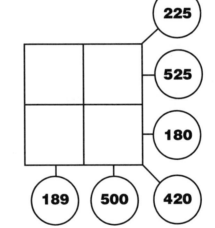

6. Factors: 11, 21, 24, 25

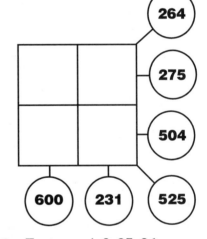

7. Factors: 9, 23, 26, 27

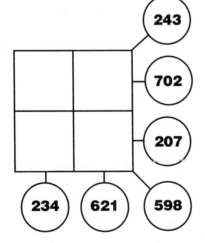

8. Factors: 21, 22, 28, 29

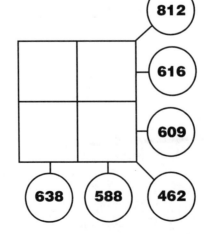

9. Factors: 4, ?, 25, 26

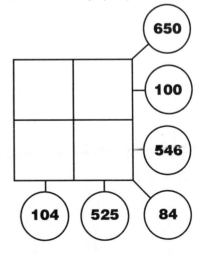

Independent Activity

Finding Products A

Use these factors to create a multiplication equation for each description.

12	27	33	56	75	81

1. _____
even product between 350 and 400

2. _____
4-digit product that's a multiple of 10

3. _____
odd product

4. _____
greatest possible even product

5. _____
4-digit product that's a multiple of 3

6. _____
odd product greater than 5,000

Use these factors to create a multiplication equation for each description.

18	23	49	65	78	92

7. _____
greatest possible odd product

8. _____
odd product less than 1,500

9. _____
product between 1,500 and 2,000

10. _____
even product between 2,000 and 2,500

11. _____
least possible even product

12. _____
even product less than 500

Date _____

Skill Check 11

 STOP Don't start yet. Star each problem that may have a multiple of ten for its answer.

1. $80 \times 7 =$ _____

2. $510 \times 6 =$ _____

3. 47
$\times 9$

4. 66
$\times 4$

5. 57
$\times 4$

6. $(3 \times 70) - 20 =$ _____

7. 464
$\times 2$

8. 507
$\times 8$

9. 36
$\times 50$

10. $500 - (32 \times 3) =$ _____

 Go On What other number belongs in this group? Explain your reasoning.

240	120	
		180
	420	

Date _____

Skill Check 12

 STOP Don't start yet. Star a problem that may have an answer greater than 2,000.

1. $70 \times 5 =$ _____

2. $620 \times 4 =$ _____

3. 58
$\times 7$

4. 77
$\times 6$

5. 49
$\times 5$

6. $(6 \times 40) - 30 =$ _____

7. 541
$\times 5$

8. 607
$\times 7$

9. 53
$\times 30$

10. $400 - (44 \times 2) =$ _____

Go On Write two different multiplication equations that have an answer of 4,800. Describe your approach.

Finding Tic-Tac-Toes B

Complete the equations. Then find the tic-tac-toe for each grid. Find the row, column, or diagonal with three numbers matching answers from the equations.

1.

49	25	143
111	74	206
120	151	62

$200 - (6 \times 23) =$ _____

$(4 \times 24) + 15 =$ _____

_____ $+ (29 \times 5) = 170$

$(9 \times 22) + 8 =$ _____

_____ $- (3 \times 34) = 18$

$301 - (36 \times 7) =$ _____

2.

181	72	97
215	48	126
83	50	18

$300 - (42 \times 6) =$ _____

$(5 \times 37) + 30 =$ _____

$(4 \times 53) - 115 =$ _____

_____ $+ (44 \times 9) = 414$

_____ $- (6 \times 27) = 19$

$330 - (35 \times 8) =$ _____

3.

87	29	340
195	103	68
246	22	202

$310 - (6 \times 48) =$ _____

$(3 \times 57) +$ _____ $= 200$

$(64 \times 5) - 125 =$ _____

$28 + (8 \times 39) =$ _____

$(9 \times 29) - 15 =$ _____

_____ $- (4 \times 19) = 126$

4.

183	86	209
95	62	37
124	91	155

$303 - (7 \times 38) =$ _____

$(3 \times 42) + 57 =$ _____

$(76 \times 4) -$ _____ $= 180$

$(6 \times 28) +$ _____ $= 259$

$(29 \times 8) - 23 =$ _____

____ $+ (9 \times 36) = 386$

Fun Fact: Five times the sum of the numbers in the tic-tac-toe row for #4 equals the year of the first international space mission.

Products Galore B

Arrange the factors to make each product.

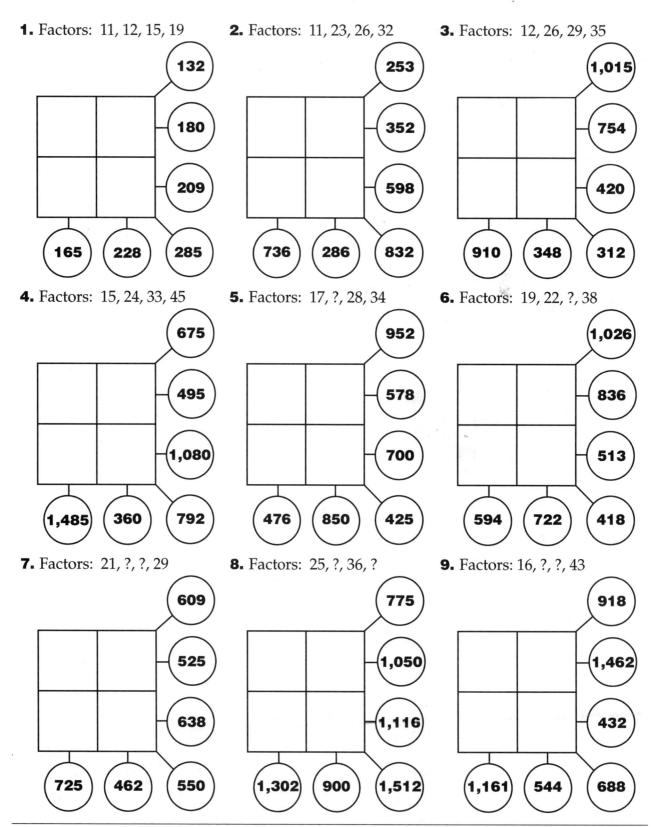

1. Factors: 11, 12, 15, 19

132
180
209
165   228   285

2. Factors: 11, 23, 26, 32

253
352
598
736   286   832

3. Factors: 12, 26, 29, 35

1,015
754
420
910   348   312

4. Factors: 15, 24, 33, 45

675
495
1,080
1,485   360   792

5. Factors: 17, ?, 28, 34

952
578
700
476   850   425

6. Factors: 19, 22, ?, 38

1,026
836
513
594   722   418

7. Factors: 21, ?, ?, 29

609
525
638
725   462   550

8. Factors: 25, ?, 36, ?

775
1,050
1,116
1,302   900   1,512

9. Factors: 16, ?, ?, 43

918
1,462
432
1,161   544   688

Finding Products B

Use these factors to create a multiplication equation for each description.

| 19 | 28 | 43 | 55 | 71 | 94 | 110 |

1. _____
even product between 1,600 and 2,000

2. _____
product between 1,000 and 2,000 that's a multiple of 10

3. _____
odd product

4. _____
least possible odd product

5. _____
4-digit product that's a multiple of 5

6. _____
even product between 6,000 and 7,500

Use these factors to create a multiplication equation for each description.

| 15 | 29 | 32 | 47 | 68 | 84 | 105 |

7. _____
greatest possible even product

8. _____
4-digit product that's a multiple of 3

9. _____
product between 1,500 and 2,000

10. _____
even product between 2,000 and 2,500

11. _____
least possible even product

12. _____
odd product between 1,000 and 1,500

Grade 5

Products Galore C

Arrange the factors to make each product.

1. Factors: 15, 23, 36, 44

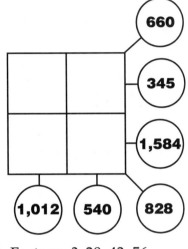

660
345
1,584
1,012 540 828

2. Factors: 18, 31, 35, 52

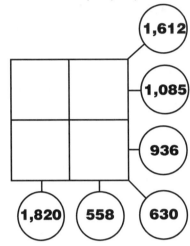

1,612
1,085
936
1,820 558 630

3. Factors: 21, ?, 29, 36

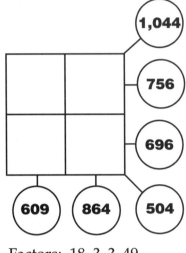

1,044
756
696
609 864 504

4. Factors: ?, 28, 43, 56

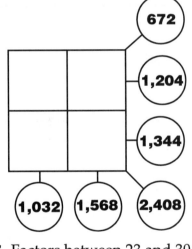

672
1,204
1,344
1,032 1,568 2,408

5. Factors: 25, ?, 39, ?

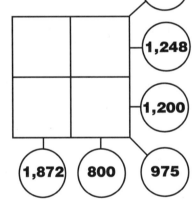

1,536
1,248
1,200
1,872 800 975

6. Factors: 18, ?, ?, 49

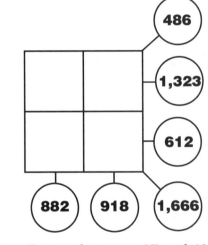

486
1,323
612
882 918 1,666

7. Factors between 23 and 30

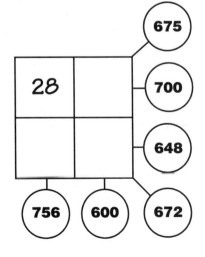

675
700
648
756 600 672

8. Factors between 25 and 34

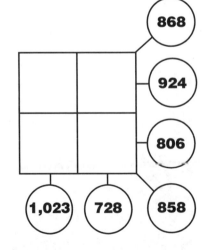

868
924
806
1,023 728 858

9. Factors between 27 and 40

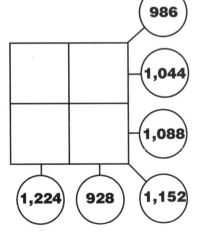

986
1,044
1,088
1,224 928 1,152

Independent Activity

Division

Unaligned Products

Warm-up

Think about the number 740. Is it divisible by 3? by 5? by 6? by 20? Explain how you know.

Number of Players: 2

Goal: Try not to cover three numbers in a row.

Materials: *Unaligned Products* gameboard (page 41)
Markers in 2 colors (9 of each color)
Calculator (optional)

Game Rules

1. The first player picks two factors. He or she picks one factor from each row in the Choices box. Both players use pencil and paper or a calculator to find the product. The first player covers the product on the gameboard.

Choices:			
3	5	6	20
56	81	148	217

    Example: The first player picks 5 and 81 and says, "5 times 81." Both players find the product. The first player covers the product, 405, on the gameboard.

2. Play continues, with players choosing factors so the products are not next to their own markers on the board. Each product may be used only one time.

3. The game ends when a player covers three in a row. That player loses the game. The row can go across, down, or diagonally.

Make It Harder: Try not to place four markers in any way that neighbors share a side. Sample arrangements to avoid:

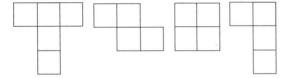

$$\begin{array}{r} 81 \\ \times\ 5 \\ \hline 405 \end{array}$$

1,120	280	444	651
405	1,302	243	2,960
168	336	1,620	888
1,085	740	4,340	486

Unaligned Products

Choices:			
3	5	6	20
56	81	148	217

1,120	**280**	**444**	**651**
405	**1,302**	**243**	**2,960**
168	**336**	**1,620**	**888**
1,085	**740**	**4,340**	**486**

Date _____

Skill Check 13

 Don't start yet. Star a problem that may have a 3-digit answer.

1. $44 \div 5 =$ _____

2. $53 \div 6 =$ _____

3. $4\overline{)300}$

4. $6\overline{)435}$

5. $8\overline{)373}$

6. $30\overline{)990}$

7. $(140 \div 5) + 4 =$ _____

8. _____ $\div 6 = 27$ R3

9. $(168 \div 4) - 3 =$ _____

10. $243 \div$ _____ $= 60$ R _____

 Use division and one other operation to make these equations true.

$70 \bigcirc (292 \bigcirc 4) = 143$ $280 \bigcirc (12 \bigcirc 5) = 40$

Date _____

Skill Check 14

 Don't start yet. Star three problems that may have remainders.

1. $36 \div 7 =$ _____

2. $62 \div 8 =$ _____

3. $5\overline{)280}$

4. $7\overline{)411}$

5. $9\overline{)337}$

6. $20\overline{)940}$

7. $(172 \div 4) + 6 =$ _____

8. _____ $\div 8 = 23$ R2

9. $(246 \div 6) - 5 =$ _____

10. $327 \div$ _____ $= 65$ R _____

 How many weeks are in 322 days?

Division Estimates

Use compatible numbers to estimate each quotient.

1. $3\overline{)1{,}947}$ **2.** $5\overline{)3{,}482}$ **3.** $6\overline{)3{,}265}$ **4.** $8\overline{)868}$

5. $4\overline{)3{,}577}$ **6.** $7\overline{)2{,}294}$ **7.** $6\overline{)3{,}807}$ **8.** $9\overline{)3{,}375}$

9. $40\overline{)22{,}643}$ **10.** $80\overline{)19{,}352}$ **11.** $90\overline{)8{,}671}$ **12.** $30\overline{)25{,}017}$

13. $70\overline{)65{,}463}$

Use this key with your answers from above to identify the type of scientist who studies birds.

100 = **I**   200 = **G**   300 = **H**   400 = **L**   500 = **N**

600 = **O**   700 = **R**   800 = **S**   900 = **T**

___ ___ ___ ___ ___ ___ ___ ___ ___ ___ ___ ___ ___
1   2   3   4   5   6   7   8   9   10   11   12   13

Trying Out the Divisibility Rules A

1.

Divisible by 2:		28	12		Not Divisible by 2:		23		
70	306	254	578		19	51	35	227	439

A number is divisible by 2 if _____

_____ .

Circle the numbers divisible by 2:   127   364   1,500   731   836

2.

Divisible by 5:		35	95		Not Divisible by 5:		36		
60	215	340	155		42	78	61	296	114

A number is divisible by 5 if _____

_____ .

Circle the numbers divisible by 5:   716   325   1,300   710   829

3.

Divisible by 10:		30	70		Not Divisible by 10:		35		
90	260	150	600		71	94	53	182	246

A number is divisible by 10 if _____

_____ .

Circle the numbers divisible by 10:   265   730   800   496   1,010

4.

Divisible by 3:		60	201		Not Divisible by 3:		49		
432	324	582	1,407		16	82	157	640	2,033

A number is divisible by 3 if _____

_____ .

Circle the numbers that are divisible by 3:   543   918   520   271   5,100

Independent Activity

Divisibility Paths A

Use the divisibility rules. Identify and shade the multiples that fit the rule next to each chart. Then draw a line through shaded cells to form a path from one side of the chart to another.

Multiples of 3

784	615	943	373	462	166
201	4,032	828	521	540	734
892	649	1,524	484	1,390	632
626	946	303	681	1,764	215
720	238	2,142	478	710	1,907
868	418	3,213	579	876	565
2,853	1,156	807	1,664	658	1,553

Multiples of 9

117	284	748	469	720	346
444	868	873	225	342	578
657	1,509	1,521	646	926	405
367	2,764	2,413	1,323	278	4,014
546	747	2,826	891	3,486	676
1,435	8,019	2,616	964	612	6,140
5,267	6,903	849	3,044	785	4,334

Skill Check 15

STOP Don't start yet. Star any problem that may not have a remainder.

1. $47 \div 6 =$ _____   **2.** $50 \div 7 =$ _____

3. $3\overline{)252}$ **4.** $7\overline{)389}$ **5.** $8\overline{)427}$ **6.** $30\overline{)870}$

7. $(148 \div 4) + 4 =$ _____   **8.** _____ $\div 7 = 32$ R5

9. $(305 \div 5) - 6 =$ _____   **10.** $213 \div$ _____ $= 53$ R _____

Go On Use division and one other operation to make each equation true.

$68 \bigcirc (246 \bigcirc 3) = 150$ $480 \bigcirc (14 \bigcirc 6) = 60$

Skill Check 16

STOP Don't start yet. Star any problem that may a 2-digit quotient.

1. $37 \div 8 =$ _____   **2.** $49 \div 6 =$ _____

3. $6\overline{)228}$ **4.** $5\overline{)327}$ **5.** $9\overline{)375}$ **6.** $40\overline{)920}$

7. $(162 \div 3) + 5 =$ _____   **8.** _____ $\div 6 = 34$ R4

9. $(288 \div 4) - 5 =$ _____   **10.** $289 \div$ _____ $= 57$ R _____

Go On How many hours are in 960 minutes?

Trying Out the Divisibility Rules B

1.

Divisible by 9:		360	261
495	585	2,934	4,015

Not Divisible by 9:			123	
481	642	793	2,014	6,568

A number is divisible by 9 if _____

_____ .

Circle the numbers divisible by 9:   414   721   1,080   639   527

2.

Divisible by 6:		72	132
504	426	780	1,734

Not Divisible by 6:			63	
92	143	272	310	1,400

A number is divisible by 6 if _____

_____ .

Circle the numbers divisible by 6:   516   142   281   684   1,320

3.

Divisible by 4:		124	216
336	500	984	1,712

Not Divisible by 4:			182	
438	318	502	2,306	1,854

A number is divisible by 4 if _____

_____ .

Circle the numbers divisible by 4:   218   380   504   1,500   174

4.

Divisible by 8:		168	256
320	564	1,888	5,640

Not Divisible by 8:			142	
364	206	516	9,428	1,452

A number is divisible by 8 if _____

_____ .

Circle the numbers divisible by 8:   720   324   1,200   820   656

Divisibility Paths B

Use the divisibility rules. Identify and shade the multiples that fit the rule next to each chart. Then draw a line through shaded cells to form a path from one side of the chart to another.

Multiples of 4

504	214	192	280	142	636
348	521	306	824	438	230
618	413	2,708	400	722	934
826	1,699	572	802	325	312
700	652	928	3,215	647	4,017
2,461	1,300	750	5,229	788	3,032
3,050	1,836	3,362	546	2,340	2,258

Multiples of 6

413	640	346	132	272	249
264	108	711	282	846	161
723	636	225	454	114	327
318	195	372	2,500	654	518
4,132	357	1,244	1,356	270	3,534
236	1,428	570	2,118	3,035	524
3,526	3,042	1,630	460	2,218	2,316

Independent Activity

Interconnecting Divisions

Complete the interconnecting problems. Make every division sentence true.
Write a number in each blank space.

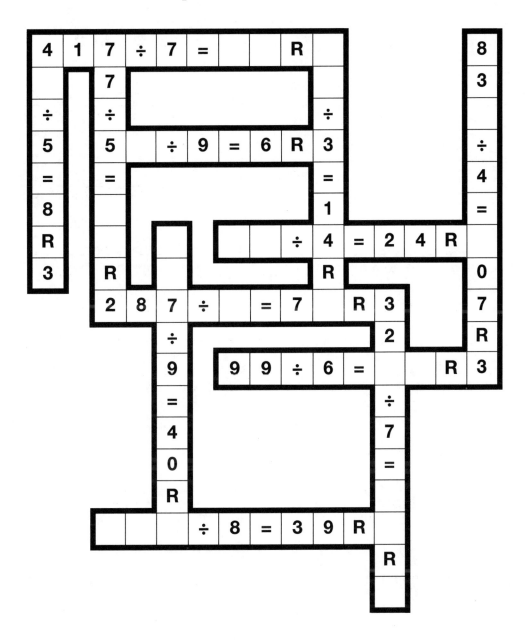

Fun Fact: The sum of the digits in all of your answers equals the number of weeks in two years.

Finding Quotients

Use the divisors and dividends to create a division equation for each description.

Divisors

| 4 | 5 | 7 | 20 |

Dividends

| 70 | 210 | 250 | 500 |

1. _____
   least quotient

2. _____
   quotient that's a multiple of 10

3. _____
   greatest quotient

4. _____
   quotient with a remainder over 6

5. _____
   even quotient with no remainder

6. _____
   quotient with an odd remainder

Use the divisors and dividends to create a division equation for each description.

Divisors

| 3 | 6 | 9 | 30 |

Dividends

| 245 | 536 | 924 | 2,700 |

7. _____
   least quotient

8. _____
   3-digit quotient with no remainder

9. _____
   quotient with no remainder

10. _____
    quotient with a remainder over 20

11. _____
    quotient with an odd remainder

12. _____
    greatest quotient with a remainder

Independent Activity

Fractions

Remember to play this game a few times. Your work often gets better when these games are played again a few days later.

Remember to date these Skill Checks so you can see improvement as you practice. The STOP activity helps you get ready for each Skill Check. Skill Check 17 should be done as you begin the section, and Skill Check 20 should be done as you end your work with this section.

These practice pages are designed to help you work faster and solve problems more accurately. Be sure to get feedback on how you're doing before starting another practice page.

Fraction Tic-Tac-Toe

Warm-up
What is the sum of $\frac{6}{8}$, $\frac{3}{6}$, and $\frac{1}{2}$? Explain your answer.

Number of Players: 4 (2 on each team)

Goal: Cover three fractions in a row that have a sum of $1\frac{1}{2}$.

Materials: *Fraction Tic-Tac-Toe* gameboard (page 53)
Markers in 2 colors (10 of each color)

Game Rules

1. Team A covers a fraction on the gameboard with one of their markers.

2. Team B covers a fraction with one of their markers.

3. Teams take turns. They try to cover three fractions in a row that total $1\frac{1}{2}$.

   Example: Team A covers $\frac{3}{6}$. Team B covers $\frac{1}{2}$. Team A covers $\frac{3}{4}$, hoping to cover $\frac{2}{8}$ on their next turn.

4. The first team to cover three fractions in a row with a total sum of $1\frac{1}{2}$ wins the game.

Make It Harder: Teams try not to cover three fractions in a row that total $1\frac{1}{2}$.

Don't Forget: Play this game over and over. It will help you do better on skill checks and independent practice pages.

$\frac{1}{4}$	$\frac{3}{6}$	$\frac{1}{2}$	$\frac{4}{8}$	$\frac{2}{4}$
$\frac{3}{4}$	$\frac{2}{4}$	$\frac{1}{4}$	$\frac{1}{2}$	$\frac{3}{4}$
$\frac{1}{2}$	$\frac{2}{8}$	$\frac{3}{6}$	$\frac{3}{4}$	$\frac{2}{8}$
$\frac{2}{8}$	$\frac{3}{4}$	$\frac{6}{8}$	$\frac{1}{4}$	$\frac{3}{6}$

$\frac{3}{6} + \frac{3}{4} + ? = 1\frac{1}{2}$

Fraction Tic-Tac-Toe

$\frac{2}{8} + \frac{1}{2} + ? = 1\frac{1}{2}$

Make $1\frac{1}{2}$

$\frac{1}{4}$	$\frac{3}{6}$	$\frac{1}{2}$	$\frac{4}{8}$	$\frac{2}{4}$
$\frac{3}{4}$	$\frac{2}{4}$	$\frac{1}{4}$	$\frac{1}{2}$	$\frac{3}{4}$
$\frac{1}{2}$	$\frac{2}{8}$	$\frac{3}{6}$	$\frac{3}{4}$	$\frac{2}{8}$
$\frac{2}{8}$	$\frac{3}{4}$	$\frac{6}{8}$	$\frac{1}{4}$	$\frac{3}{6}$

Date _____

Skill Check 17

STOP Don't start yet. Star a problem that may have an answer equal to a whole number.

1. Circle the fractions that are less than $\frac{1}{2}$. $\frac{4}{9}$ $\frac{3}{5}$ $\frac{1}{4}$ $\frac{7}{13}$ $\frac{3}{7}$

2. $\frac{4}{8}$ = ____   **3.** $\frac{2}{10}$ = ____   **4.** $\frac{2}{5} + \frac{3}{5}$ = ____   **5.** $\frac{7}{8} - \frac{5}{8}$ = ____

6. Order these fractions from least to greatest. $\frac{1}{2}$ $\frac{3}{8}$ $\frac{4}{7}$

_____   _____   _____
    least   greatest

7. $\frac{5}{9} + \frac{1}{3}$ = ____   **8.** $\frac{11}{12} + \frac{5}{12}$ = ____   **9.** $\frac{5}{6} - \frac{1}{2}$ = ____

10. If ■ = $\frac{1}{4}$, then ■ ■ = ____ and ■ ■ ■ ■ ■ = ____ .

Go On What other fraction belongs? Describe your rule.

| $\frac{6}{8}$ | $\frac{12}{16}$ | $\frac{15}{20}$ | $\frac{3}{4}$ |

Date _____

Skill Check 18

STOP Don't start yet. Star a problem that may have an answer less than $\frac{1}{2}$.

1. Circle the fractions that are greater than $\frac{3}{4}$. $\frac{2}{3}$ $\frac{13}{16}$ $\frac{5}{6}$ $\frac{11}{12}$ $\frac{5}{8}$

2. $\frac{3}{12}$ = ____   **3.** $\frac{3}{9}$ = ____   **4.** $\frac{3}{6} + \frac{1}{6}$ = ____   **5.** $\frac{7}{10} - \frac{3}{10}$ = ____

6. Order these fractions from least to greatest. $\frac{2}{3}$ $\frac{5}{9}$ $\frac{3}{8}$

_____   _____   _____
    least   greatest

7. $\frac{3}{4} + \frac{1}{8}$ = ____   **8.** $\frac{3}{4} - \frac{5}{12}$ = ____   **9.** $\frac{5}{9} + \frac{7}{9}$ = ____

10. If ▲ = $\frac{1}{6}$, then ▲ ▲ ▲ = ____ and ▲ ▲ ▲ ▲ ▲ = ____ .

Go On What comes next? $\frac{1}{4}$, 1, $1\frac{3}{4}$, ____, ____, ____
Describe the pattern.

If... Then... A

Solve each of the following problems. The first one is done for you.

If ▲ = $\frac{1}{4}$, then . . .

1.   ▲▲ = $\frac{1}{2}$ **2.**   ▲▲▲▲▲▲ = _____

3.   ▲▲▲▲▲ = _____   **4.**   ▲▲▲ = _____

If ★★★ = 1, then . . .

5.   ★★ = _____   **6.**   ★★★★★★ = _____

7.   ★★★★ = _____   **8.**   ★ = _____

If ✿✿ = 1, then . . .

9.   ✿✿✿✿ = _____   **10.**   ✿✿✿✿✿ = _____

11.   ✿ = _____   **12.**   ✿✿✿ = _____

If ■■ = $\frac{1}{4}$, then . . .

13.   ■ = _____   **14.**   ■■■■■ = _____

15.   ■■■■■■■■ = _____   **16.**   ■■■■■■■■■■■■ = _____

If ❤❤❤ = 6, then . . .

17.   ❤❤ = _____   **18.**   ❤❤❤❤ = _____

19.   ❤❤❤❤❤❤ = _____   **20.**   ❤ = _____

If OOO = $\frac{1}{2}$, then . . .

21.   O = _____   **22.**   OOOOOOO = _____

23.   OO = _____   **24.**   OOOO = _____

```
 ├──┬──── ───┬──┬──┤
 A  B      C  D  E  F
```

25. If A = 0 and F = 1,   what's the value of B? _____ C? _____ D? _____

26. If A = 0 and F = $1\frac{1}{2}$,   what's the value of B? _____ D? _____ E? _____

27. If A = 0 and F = $1\frac{1}{5}$,   what's the value of B? _____ C? _____ D? _____

Independent Activity

Fraction Paths A

Draw a line to connect fractions that total the target number. You may begin and end at any number, but you may pass through a cell only once. **Hint:** More than one path might be possible.

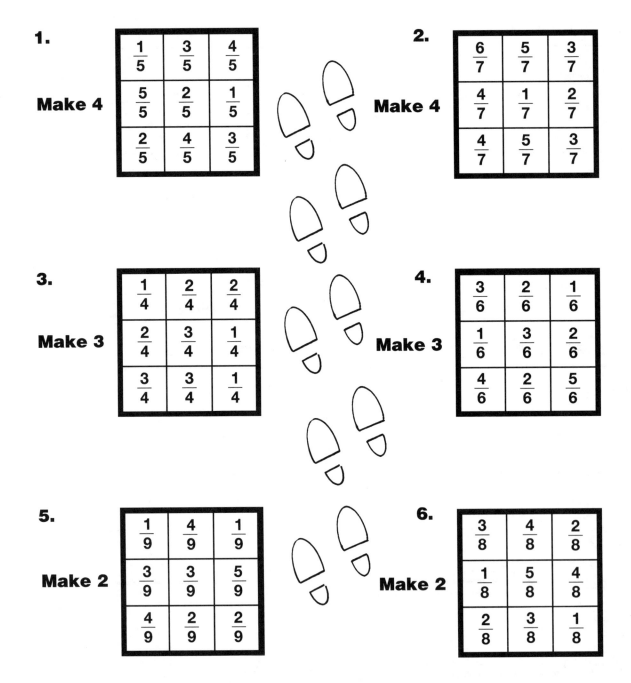

1.

Make 4

$\frac{1}{5}$	$\frac{3}{5}$	$\frac{4}{5}$
$\frac{5}{5}$	$\frac{2}{5}$	$\frac{1}{5}$
$\frac{2}{5}$	$\frac{4}{5}$	$\frac{3}{5}$

2.

Make 4

$\frac{6}{7}$	$\frac{5}{7}$	$\frac{3}{7}$
$\frac{4}{7}$	$\frac{1}{7}$	$\frac{2}{7}$
$\frac{4}{7}$	$\frac{5}{7}$	$\frac{3}{7}$

3.

Make 3

$\frac{1}{4}$	$\frac{2}{4}$	$\frac{2}{4}$
$\frac{2}{4}$	$\frac{3}{4}$	$\frac{1}{4}$
$\frac{3}{4}$	$\frac{3}{4}$	$\frac{1}{4}$

4.

Make 3

$\frac{3}{6}$	$\frac{2}{6}$	$\frac{1}{6}$
$\frac{1}{6}$	$\frac{3}{6}$	$\frac{2}{6}$
$\frac{4}{6}$	$\frac{2}{6}$	$\frac{5}{6}$

5.

Make 2

$\frac{1}{9}$	$\frac{4}{9}$	$\frac{1}{9}$
$\frac{3}{9}$	$\frac{3}{9}$	$\frac{5}{9}$
$\frac{4}{9}$	$\frac{2}{9}$	$\frac{2}{9}$

6.

Make 2

$\frac{3}{8}$	$\frac{4}{8}$	$\frac{2}{8}$
$\frac{1}{8}$	$\frac{5}{8}$	$\frac{4}{8}$
$\frac{2}{8}$	$\frac{3}{8}$	$\frac{1}{8}$

Digits to Fractions A

Use each of these displayed digits once in each equation. Create fractions to make each equation true.

| 1 | 2 | 3 | 6 |

1. $\dfrac{\square}{\square} + \dfrac{\square}{\square} = 1$

2. $\dfrac{\square}{\square} + \dfrac{\square}{\square} = \dfrac{5}{6}$

3. $\dfrac{\square}{\square} - \dfrac{\square}{\square} = 0$

4. $\dfrac{\square}{\square} - \dfrac{\square}{\square} = \dfrac{1}{2}$

| 1 | 2 | 4 | 8 |

5. $\dfrac{\square}{\square} + \dfrac{\square}{\square} = \dfrac{1}{2}$

6. $\dfrac{\square}{\square} + \dfrac{\square}{\square} = \dfrac{5}{8}$

7. $\dfrac{\square}{\square} - \dfrac{\square}{\square} = 0$

8. $\dfrac{\square}{\square} - \dfrac{\square}{\square} = \dfrac{3}{8}$

| 1 | 3 | 6 | 12 |

9. $\dfrac{\square}{\square} + \dfrac{\square}{\square} = \dfrac{5}{12}$

10. $\dfrac{\square}{\square} - \dfrac{\square}{\square} = \dfrac{5}{12}$

Date _____

Skill Check 19

STOP Don't start yet. Star a problem that may have an answer greater than one.

1. Circle the fractions that are greater than $\frac{1}{2}$. $\frac{3}{4}$ $\frac{5}{8}$ $\frac{1}{3}$ $\frac{3}{7}$ $\frac{7}{10}$

2. $\frac{5}{20} =$ _____   **3.** $\frac{6}{12} =$ _____   **4.** $\frac{5}{8} + \frac{1}{8} =$ _____   **5.** $\frac{7}{9} - \frac{2}{9} =$ _____

6. Order these fractions from least to greatest. $\frac{3}{4}$ $\frac{7}{12}$ $\frac{2}{3}$

_____   _____   _____
least   greatest

7. $\frac{1}{2} + \frac{1}{6} =$ _____   **8.** $\frac{7}{8} + \frac{3}{8} =$ _____   **9.** $\frac{7}{10} - \frac{3}{5} =$ _____

10. If $= \frac{2}{5}$, then $=$ _____ and ⬤⬤⬤⬤⬤ $=$ _____ .

Go On → What other fraction belongs?
Describe your rule.

| $\frac{2}{6}$ | $\frac{1}{3}$ | $\frac{6}{18}$ | $\frac{4}{12}$ |

Date _____

Skill Check 20

STOP Don't start yet. Star a problem that may have an answer greater than $\frac{1}{2}$.

1. Circle the fractions that are less than $\frac{2}{3}$. $\frac{1}{4}$ $\frac{3}{4}$ $\frac{5}{6}$ $\frac{7}{15}$ $\frac{7}{12}$

2. $\frac{8}{10} =$ _____   **3.** $\frac{10}{15} =$ _____   **4.** $\frac{5}{7} + \frac{2}{7} =$ _____   **5.** $\frac{4}{5} - \frac{2}{5} =$ _____

6. Order these fractions from least to greatest. $\frac{1}{3}$ $\frac{5}{6}$ $\frac{2}{9}$

_____   _____   _____
least   greatest

7. $\frac{2}{5} + \frac{3}{10} =$ _____   **8.** $\frac{3}{4} - \frac{3}{8} =$ _____   **9.** $\frac{7}{10} + \frac{7}{10} =$ _____

10. If ■ $= \frac{2}{3}$, then ■■ $=$ _____ and ■■■■ $=$ _____ .

Go On → What comes next? $6, 5\frac{1}{3}, 4\frac{2}{3},$ _____ , _____ , _____
Describe the pattern.

Skill Checks

If... Then... B

Solve each of the following problems. The first one is done for you.

If ▲ = $\frac{1}{3}$, then . . .

1. ▲▲ = $\frac{2}{3}$

2. ▲▲▲▲▲▲▲ = _____

3. ▲▲▲▲ = _____

4. ▲▲▲▲▲ = _____

If ★★★ = $\frac{3}{4}$, then . . .

5. ★ = _____

6. ★★ = _____

7. ★★★★ = _____

8. ★★★★★ = _____

If ✿✿ = 3, then . . .

9. ✿✿✿✿✿✿ = _____

10. ✿✿✿✿✿ = _____

11. ✿ = _____

12. ✿✿✿ = _____

If ■■ = $\frac{1}{2}$, then . . .

13. ■ = _____

14. ■■■■■ = _____

15. ■■■■■■■■ = _____

16. ■■■■■■■■■■■■ = _____

If ❤❤❤❤ = 8, then . . .

17. ❤❤ = _____

18. ❤❤❤ = _____

19. ❤❤❤❤❤❤ = _____

20. ❤ = _____

If ОООО = $\frac{1}{2}$, then . . .

21. О = _____

22. ОООООООО = _____

23. ОО = _____

24. ООООО = _____

```
├──┬──┬─── ─── ──┬── ──┬──┬─┤
A    B         C       D  E  F
```

25. If A = 0 and F = 1, what's the value of B? _____ D? _____ E? _____

26. If A = 0 and F = 2, what's the value of B? _____ C? _____ D? _____

27. If A = 0 and F = $1\frac{1}{3}$, what's the value of B? _____ C? _____ D? _____

Independent Activity

Fraction Paths B

Draw a line to connect fractions that total the target number. You may begin and end at any number, but you may pass through a cell only once. **Hint:** More than one path might be possible.

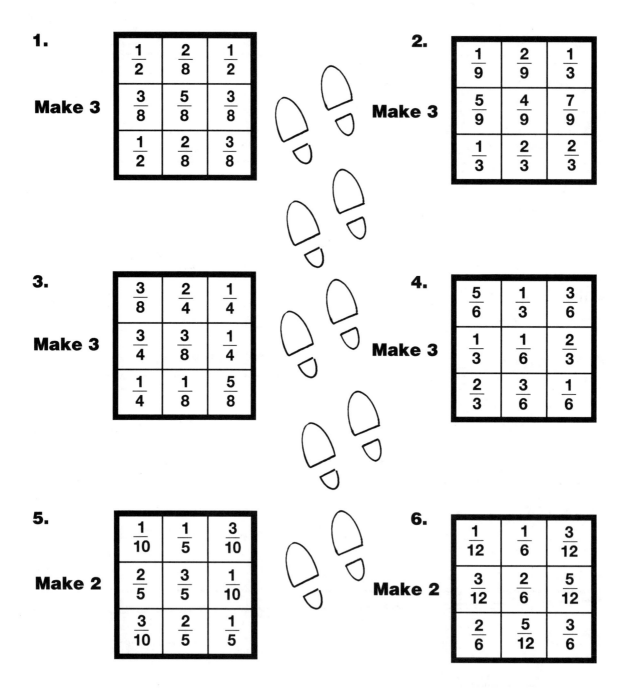

1.

Make 3

$\frac{1}{2}$	$\frac{2}{8}$	$\frac{1}{2}$
$\frac{3}{8}$	$\frac{5}{8}$	$\frac{3}{8}$
$\frac{1}{2}$	$\frac{2}{8}$	$\frac{3}{8}$

2.

Make 3

$\frac{1}{9}$	$\frac{2}{9}$	$\frac{1}{3}$
$\frac{5}{9}$	$\frac{4}{9}$	$\frac{7}{9}$
$\frac{1}{3}$	$\frac{2}{3}$	$\frac{2}{3}$

3.

Make 3

$\frac{3}{8}$	$\frac{2}{4}$	$\frac{1}{4}$
$\frac{3}{4}$	$\frac{3}{8}$	$\frac{1}{4}$
$\frac{1}{4}$	$\frac{1}{8}$	$\frac{5}{8}$

4.

Make 3

$\frac{5}{6}$	$\frac{1}{3}$	$\frac{3}{6}$
$\frac{1}{3}$	$\frac{1}{6}$	$\frac{2}{3}$
$\frac{2}{3}$	$\frac{3}{6}$	$\frac{1}{6}$

5.

Make 2

$\frac{1}{10}$	$\frac{1}{5}$	$\frac{3}{10}$
$\frac{2}{5}$	$\frac{3}{5}$	$\frac{1}{10}$
$\frac{3}{10}$	$\frac{2}{5}$	$\frac{1}{5}$

6.

Make 2

$\frac{1}{12}$	$\frac{1}{6}$	$\frac{3}{12}$
$\frac{3}{12}$	$\frac{2}{6}$	$\frac{5}{12}$
$\frac{2}{6}$	$\frac{5}{12}$	$\frac{3}{6}$

Independent Activity

Digits to Fractions B

Use each of these displayed digits once in each equation. Create fractions to make each equation true.

| 1 | 3 | 3 | 9 |

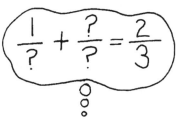

$$1.\ \frac{\square}{\square} + \frac{\square}{\square} = \frac{2}{3}$$

$$2.\ \frac{\square}{\square} + \frac{\square}{\square} = 1\frac{1}{9}$$

$$3.\ \frac{\square}{\square} - \frac{\square}{\square} = 0$$

$$4.\ \frac{\square}{\square} - \frac{\square}{\square} = \frac{8}{9}$$

Use any 4 of these displayed digits in each equation. Create fractions to make each equation true.

| 1 | 2 | 3 | 6 | 12 |

$$5.\ \frac{\square}{\square} + \frac{\square}{\square} = \frac{7}{12}$$

$$6.\ \frac{\square}{\square} + \frac{\square}{\square} = \frac{1}{2}$$

$$7.\ \frac{\square}{\square} - \frac{\square}{\square} = \frac{1}{4}$$

$$8.\ \frac{\square}{\square} + \frac{\square}{\square} = \frac{1}{6}$$

$$9.\ \frac{\square}{\square} + \frac{\square}{\square} = 2\frac{1}{2}$$

$$10.\ \frac{\square}{\square} + \frac{\square}{\square} = 4\frac{1}{3}$$

$$11.\ \frac{\square}{\square} - \frac{\square}{\square} = 1$$

$$12.\ \frac{\square}{\square} - \frac{\square}{\square} = 1\frac{5}{6}$$

Fraction Paths C

Draw a line to connect fractions that total the target number. You may begin and end at any number, but you may pass through a cell only once. **Hint:** More than one path might be possible.

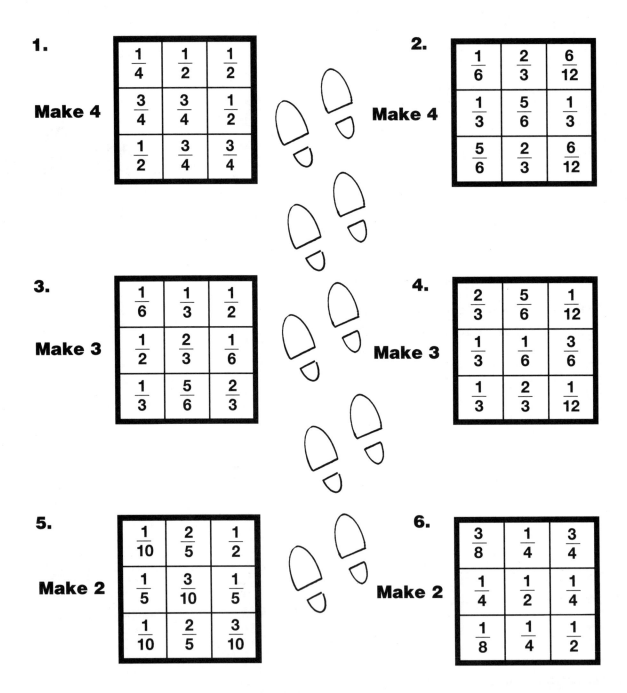

1.

Make 4

$\frac{1}{4}$	$\frac{1}{2}$	$\frac{1}{2}$
$\frac{3}{4}$	$\frac{3}{4}$	$\frac{1}{2}$
$\frac{1}{2}$	$\frac{3}{4}$	$\frac{3}{4}$

2.

Make 4

$\frac{1}{6}$	$\frac{2}{3}$	$\frac{6}{12}$
$\frac{1}{3}$	$\frac{5}{6}$	$\frac{1}{3}$
$\frac{5}{6}$	$\frac{2}{3}$	$\frac{6}{12}$

3.

Make 3

$\frac{1}{6}$	$\frac{1}{3}$	$\frac{1}{2}$
$\frac{1}{2}$	$\frac{2}{3}$	$\frac{1}{6}$
$\frac{1}{3}$	$\frac{5}{6}$	$\frac{2}{3}$

4.

Make 3

$\frac{2}{3}$	$\frac{5}{6}$	$\frac{1}{12}$
$\frac{1}{3}$	$\frac{1}{6}$	$\frac{3}{6}$
$\frac{1}{3}$	$\frac{2}{3}$	$\frac{1}{12}$

5.

Make 2

$\frac{1}{10}$	$\frac{2}{5}$	$\frac{1}{2}$
$\frac{1}{5}$	$\frac{3}{10}$	$\frac{1}{5}$
$\frac{1}{10}$	$\frac{2}{5}$	$\frac{3}{10}$

6.

Make 2

$\frac{3}{8}$	$\frac{1}{4}$	$\frac{3}{4}$
$\frac{1}{4}$	$\frac{1}{2}$	$\frac{1}{4}$
$\frac{1}{8}$	$\frac{1}{4}$	$\frac{1}{2}$

Independent Activity

Digit Cards

0	1	2	3
4	5	<u>6</u>	7
8	<u>9</u>	0	1
2	3	4	5
<u>6</u>	7	8	<u>9</u>